EXTREME SPORTS
An Imagination Library Series

SCUBA DIVING

by Carol Ryback

Gareth Stevens
Publishing

Please visit our web site at: www.garethstevens.com
For a free color catalog describing Gareth Stevens Publishing's list of high-quality books, call 1-800-542-2595 (USA) or 1-800-387-3178 (Canada).
Gareth Stevens Publishing's fax: 1-877-542-2596

Library of Congress Cataloging-in-Publication Data available upon request from publisher.
Fax (414) 336-0157 for the attention of the Publishing Records Department.

ISBN-10: 0-8368-4542-0 (lib. bdg.)
ISBN-13: 978-0-8368-4542-6 (lib. bdg.)
ISBN-10: 0-8368-4549-8 (softcover)
ISBN-13: 978-0-8368-4549-5 (softcover)

First published in 2005 by
Gareth Stevens Publishing
A Weekly Reader® Company
1 Reader's Digest Road
Pleasantville, NY 10570-7000 USA

Text: Carol Ryback
Cover design and page layout: Tammy West
Editor: JoAnn Early Macken
Photo research: Diane Laska-Swanke

Photo credits: Cover © Doug Perrine/SeaPics.com; p. 5 © Larry Benvenuti; pp. 7, 9 © C.A. Ryback; p. 11 © Graeme Teague; p. 13 © Jeff Jaskolski/SeaPics.com; p. 15 © Tim Rock/SeaPics.com; p. 17 © Davidson/gtphoto; p. 19 © David Shen/SeaPics.com; p. 21 © Nachoum/gtphoto

Printed in the United States of America

CPSIA Compliance Information: Batch #CR019110GS: For further information contact Gareth Stevens, New York, New York at 1-800-542-2595

Cover: A scuba diver explores a coral reef. The underwater plants and animals that live on the reef come in many bright colors.

TABLE OF CONTENTS

Words that appear in the glossary are printed in **boldface** type the first time they occur in the text.

GET WET!

Imagine yourself in a boat on an ocean. You can see lots of fish, plants, and rocks in the water. What else is down there?

Why not take a closer look? Do you like to swim? Maybe someday you can learn to **scuba dive**!

"Scuba" is not a normal word. It stands for "Self-Contained Underwater Breathing Apparatus." This is a fancy way of saying you breathe air from a tank that you carry as you swim underwater.

A scuba diver takes a giant step off a boat and into the water.

GOT AIR?

Maybe you know how to dive underwater for a few seconds. Soon, you come up for air because you have to breathe.

Long ago, some swimmer had an idea. He held a **hollow** stick in his mouth. The hollow stick was like a straw. It helped him get air when his head was underwater! Modern divers use a **snorkel** instead of a hollow stick. They must stay near the top of the water to breathe.

Scuba diving is different. A scuba diver goes deep underwater. She carries an air supply with her. A scuba diver often stays underwater for a long time.

Scuba diving gear helps you take a closer look at underwater objects.

GEAR DOWN

You need scuba gear from head to toe. Your dive mask is your most important piece of scuba gear. It lets you enjoy the underwater show. Swim fins give your kicks more power.

A special safety vest called a **BCD** helps you move up and down. The BCD also holds your air tank on your back. A long tube from the tank brings air to your mouth.

Your dive watch keeps time underwater. Your dive computer tells how deep you go. It also tells how much air is in your tank. You also need to carry weights to help you sink — but not too far!

Scuba divers carry all kinds of gear to keep them safe.

BE A "C" STUDENT

Owning scuba gear does not make you a scuba diver. You must earn a "C" card by taking scuba diving lessons.

A "C" card means you are a **certified** scuba diver. It is like having a diving license!

Scuba lessons teach you how to stay safe underwater. You will learn how to use the scuba gear. The lessons have three parts. First, you study in a classroom. Next, you practice scuba skills in a pool. Finally, you use scuba gear in **open water**.

Now you are swimming with the fish!

Scuba diving students learn to use scuba gear in a pool. Soon they will dive in a lake or ocean.

A SPORT WITH A VIEW

Corals are tiny animals that live and grow on top of underwater rock, called a reef. They like warm water. Corals also need lots of sunlight to grow. Underwater rock with growing corals is called a **coral reef**.

A coral reef is a good place to go scuba diving. Fish of all shapes and bright colors swim around the reef. Bigger fish, such as sharks, might visit the coral reef.

Other ocean animals hide on coral reefs. You might find a shrimp, an **eel**, or an octopus. Look closely, but do not touch!

What would you hope to see on a coral reef?

Many creatures live on coral reefs. The corals, sponges, and other sea animals and plants create colorful underwater wonders that are fun to visit.

IN A TIGHT SPACE

All scuba divers must be very careful. Some types of scuba diving are extremely dangerous. Scuba divers who explore tight spaces or inside sunken objects need special lessons.

Divers who go into shipwrecks, enter caves, or dive under ice always carry special safety gear. They might carry extra air tanks. They often use ropes to mark their way out. They take special flashlights to see where they are going.

Some scuba divers enter shipwrecks to see where the sailors slept. Scuba divers in underwater caves might see fish that glow in the dark! Ice divers see underwater icicles!

Whoever thought about scuba diving in an airplane? Divers who plan to enter large sunken objects must learn special safety skills.

SCUBA? DO!

Many scuba divers are **scientists**. They scuba dive to study fish and underwater plants. Some scientists might sit on the bottom of the ocean and draw maps.

Other scuba divers build bridges or fix underwater pipes. Rescue divers scuba dive to save lives. A sailor might use scuba gear to check for holes if his boat gets a leak.

Treasure divers look for sunken ships that carried gold, silver, or jewels! Underwater photographers capture beautiful pictures of ocean life.

Maybe you will work underwater someday!

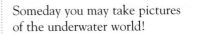

Someday you may take pictures of the underwater world!

SCUBA SEA STARS

Some scuba divers are famous. Jacques Cousteau (jawk COOS-toe) helped invent modern scuba diving gear. At first, he went scuba diving mostly to catch fish and have fun. Soon, he began to scuba dive all around the world.

Cousteau saw dying coral reefs in many parts of the oceans. He wrote many books about the oceans. He also made underwater movies about ocean life.

Eugenie Clark and Sylvia Earle are two other famous scuba divers. They are **oceanographers**. They study the ocean and its creatures. Eugenie and Sylvia also teach others about the ocean world.

Oceanographer Eugenie Clark uses her scuba diving skills to study ocean life.

SEA FOR YOURSELF

Why should you scuba dive? Scuba diving is fun. It is also exciting. You will see underwater wonders that few people ever see. Scuba diving also helps you learn about ocean life.

What is one of the best reasons to learn to scuba dive? You can go scuba diving your whole life. Imagine that — you could someday scuba dive with your grandchildren!

Make sure you are a strong swimmer. Get scuba certified. Take advanced scuba lessons. Always follow scuba diving safety rules and never dive alone. Learn all you can about the oceans and sea life.

So let's go scuba diving — the oceans are waiting!

A scuba diver glides underneath a **manta ray**. Manta rays belong to the shark family of ocean animals. They are harmless — and toothless!

MORE TO READ AND VIEW

Books (Nonfiction) *Coral Reef: A Life That Never Sleeps.* Mary M. Cerullo. (Dutton Books)

Coral Reef Coloring Book. Ruth Soffer. (Dover)

Hello, Fish: Visiting the Coral Reef. Sylvia A. Earle. (National Geographic)

How to Hide an Octopus and Other Sea Creatures. Ruth Heller. (Grosset and Dunlap)

The Incredible Coral Reef: Another Active-Learning Book for Kids. Toni Albert. (Trickle Creek Books)

Under the Sea From A to Z. Anne Doubilet. (Random House)

Books (Fiction) *Mutley Goes Diving. Mutley's True Adventures* (series). Gene Alba. (Heian International)

DVDs and Videos *The Best of: John Pennekamp Coral Reef State Park.* (International Video Products)

Coral Reef Adventure. (Image Entertainment)

WEB SITES

Web sites change frequently, but the following web sites should last awhile. You can also search Google (*www.google.com*) or Yahooligans! (*www.yahooligans.com*) for more information about scuba diving. Some keywords to help your search include: *ActionQuest, Broadreach, Cousteau Society, diving bells, Navy SEALS, scuba diving history, underwater archaeology.*

www.enchantedlearning.com/ biomes/coralreef/coralreef.shtml
Learn about life on a coral reef. Follow links to information on reef creatures. Print out your favorites to color and study.

www.flmnh.ufl.edu/fish/south florida/games/sharkwordsearch. html
Solve a shark word-search puzzle. Print out your own copy and find the names of the many different kinds of sharks that swim the world.

www.seasky.org/reeflife/sea2a.html
Sponges are not just for cleaning your sink! Learn how these simple animals help keep the water clean. See many different shapes and colors of sponges.

www.seaworld.org/animal- info/info-books/coral/classroom- activities-gc.htm
Grow your own coral! Ask an adult to help you make your own private coral reef.

GLOSSARY

You can find these words on the pages listed. Reading a word in a sentence helps you understand it even better.

BCD — **B**ouyancy **C**ompensator **D**evice, a piece of scuba gear that looks like a vest. It helps control how much a diver floats or sinks. It also holds the air tank. 8

certified — having studied something and earned a licensed to do it. 10, 20

coral reef — an underwater structure formed by the buildup of millions of skeletons of tiny coral animals. A coral reef is covered with a layer of living corals. 12

eel — a snakelike ocean animal. 12

hollow — empty inside. 6

manta ray — an ocean animal that is related to sharks but is toothless. It looks like a big flat fish with "wings" and a tail. 20

mouthpiece — a part that fits in the mouth. 8

oceanographer — a scientist who studies the oceans and ocean life. 18

open water — a body of water with a surface that is open to the sky. 10

scuba dive — to swim underwater while carrying air in a container. 4, 6, 14, 16, 20

snorkel — a tube used for breathing while underwater. 6

INDEX